Save Water

Kay Barnham

 Crabtree Publishing Company
www.crabtreebooks.com

Crabtree Publishing Company

www.crabtreebooks.com

Editors: Penny Worms, Molly Aloian, Michael Hodge
Senior Design Manager: Rosamund Saunders
Designer: Ben Ruocco, Tall Tree Ltd

Photo Credits:
Alamy: p. 14 (Ethel Davies), p. 20 (mediacolour's), p. 25 (plainpicture/Usbeck.P), p. 29 (John Walmsley). Corbis images: p. 7 (Geray Sweeney), p. 18 (Kontos Yannis), p. 22 (Edward Bock), p. 26 (Johnny Buzzerio). Ecoscene: p. 5 (NASA), p. 15 (Angela Hampton), p. 16 (Rosemary Greenwood), p. 17 (Paul Ferraby), p. 24 (Angela Hampton), p. 28 (Stephen Coyne). Getty images: p. 4 (Peter Essick), p. 13 (Gavin Hellier), p. 23 (Kroeger/Gross). Rex Features: p. 10 (Sipa Press). Photolibrary: cover and p. 27 (Peter Fogg). Wayland Picture Library: title page and p. 12, p. 6, p. 8, p. 9, p. 11, p. 19, p. 21.

Library and Archives Canada Cataloguing in Publication

Barnham, Kay
   Save water / Kay Barnham.

(Environment action)
Includes index.
ISBN 978-0-7787-3661-5 (bound).--ISBN 978-0-7787-3671-4 (pbk.)

   1. Water conservation--Juvenile literature. 2. Water-supply--Juvenile
literature. I. Title. II. Series: Barnham, Kay. Environment action.

TD388.B37 2007   j333.91'16   C2007-904687-8

Library of Congress Cataloging-in-Publication Data

Barnham, Kay.
   Save water / Kay Barnham.
     p. cm. -- (Environment action)
   Includes index.
   ISBN-13: 978-0-7787-3661-5 (rlb)
   ISBN-10: 0-7787-3661-X (rlb)
   ISBN-13: 978-0-7787-3671-4 (pb)
   ISBN-10: 0-7787-3671-7 (pb)
   1. Water conservation--Juvenile literature. I. Title. II. Series.

   TD495.B37 2008
   333.91'16--dc22

            2007030002

Crabtree Publishing Company

www.crabtreebooks.com   1-800-387-7650

Published in Canada
Crabtree Publishing
616 Welland Ave.
St. Catharines, Ontario
L2M 5V6

Published in the United States
Crabtree Publishing
PMB16A
350 Fifth Ave., Suite 3308
New York, NY 10118

Published by CRABTREE PUBLISHING COMPANY
Copyright © **2008**

Contents

All about water

Water has no taste, no smell, and no color.
At first glance, you might think that water is
quite boring. Water is actually very important!
Without water, we could not survive.

△ More than half of your body is made of
water. You lose water every day. The water
you lose must be replaced by more water.

△ This picture shows Earth from space. The green and brown areas are land. The blue areas are water. The white areas are clouds and ice. There is a lot of water on Earth!

Much of the Earth's **surface** is covered in water. Water is found in oceans, seas, lakes, rivers, and streams. Ice and snow are made of frozen water.

The water cycle

The amount of water on Earth never changes. It does not increase or decrease. Water moves from place to place. Your drinking water may have once tumbled down a **waterfall** on the other side of the world.

△ Water is constantly moving. This water will eventually reach an ocean.

The **water cycle** describes the way that water moves from place to place.

- The sun warms ocean water, causing **water vapor** to rise into the air.
- As water vapor rises and cools, it turns into tiny **droplets** of water.
- The droplets of water form clouds.
- Wind blows the clouds over land.
- When the droplets of water in the clouds become too big and heavy, they fall as rain.
- Water flows down streams and rivers until it reaches oceans again.

▽ **When these clouds blow toward high ground, rain will fall.**

Why save water?

Why do we need to save water? The answer is simple—there is plenty of water on Earth, but we can only use a small amount of it. It is important that we conserve all of the water on Earth.

△ The salty water in oceans cannot be used for drinking or washing. Drinking a lot of ocean water could make you very sick.

△ Each person on Earth needs a lot of water.

There is another problem. Earth's **population** is growing bigger every year, but there is no extra water. By using less water, we can make sure that there is enough water for everyone.

A cleaner world

Pollution is dirty or unhealthy land, air, or water. It can cause many problems and harm people, animals, and plants. Many people are concerned about pollution and do their best to stop it. They want Earth to be a cleaner, healthier place.

 When **chemicals** from **factories** and **sewers** pour into rivers and streams, the water becomes polluted.

The dirty smoke that comes from factories does not just pollute the air. Clouds carry the pollution to different places and polluted rain falls to the ground. This polluted rain is called **acid rain**. Acid rain can **destroy** forests.

△ When oil tankers spill oil into oceans, the oil pollutes coastlines. It takes a lot of effort to clean up all of the oil.

Surface water

Most of the water that we use comes from Earth's surface. Fresh water flows in rivers and streams, and is stored in lakes. It is cleaned and then **piped** to homes, offices, factories, and farms.

◁ The water in this river is pumped to wherever it is needed.

A **dam** is a strong wall built across a river **valley**. Instead of flowing to oceans, the water is trapped behind the dam. This water can be used when the weather is dry and water supplies are low.

△ The water held back by a dam is called a **reservoir**. Many animals live in reservoirs.

Ground water

Some of the water that we use does not come from rivers, streams, or reservoirs. Some water soaks into the ground. It is hidden below the surface in gaps between layers of rock. This water is called **ground water**.

△ There is a lot of water stored in underground pools like this one.

It costs more to use ground water than it does to use surface water. Ground water is harder to reach than a river or a reservoir is. A hole must be dug down to the level of the water. The water is then pumped to the surface.

▽ A **well** is a deep hole that reaches down to the water underground. Water is brought up to the surface in a bucket.

Waste water

When water is washed down the sink or **flushed** down the toilet, it cannot be poured straight back into a river or an ocean. It is too dirty. The dirty water travels down pipes to a **wastewater treatment works**, where it is cleaned.

△ Toilet water is cleaned at sewage plants.

After being cleaned and treated, the water is clean enough to be pumped back into rivers and oceans.

At the wastewater treatment works, the water is cleaned. It runs through **coarse** layers of stones and then finer layers of sand. The stones and sand remove waste. Any remaining **germs** are killed with a special type of light or by chemicals.

FACT!

If waste water was not treated, it would harm plants, animals, and the **environment**.

Ocean water

Ocean water is very salty. People cannot use it for drinking, cooking, washing, or watering crops. People living on small islands and in hot, dry countries may be surrounded by ocean water, but they have very little fresh water. They have special ways of removing salt from ocean water.

△ People on **submarines** get the fresh water that they use on board by removing salt from ocean water.

When water vapor rises from oceans to form clouds, the salt is left behind in the oceans. As a result, rain is always fresh water.

△ The next time it rains, imagine where the water might have come from. Maybe it came from the Pacific Ocean or the Atlantic Ocean!

Turn it off!

The easiest way to save water is to turn the tap off. Millions of liters of clean, fresh water disappear down drains every day. Before the water can be used again, it must be pumped away, cleaned, and then pumped back. Turning taps off saves water and energy!

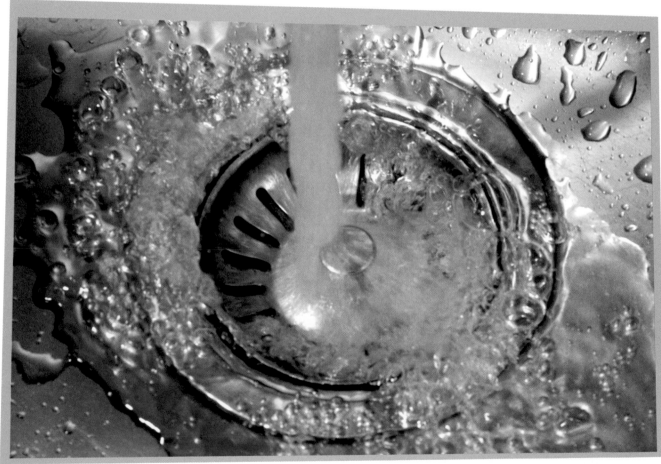

△ If you leave the tap running while you brush your teeth, you could use as much as six liters of water.

Did you know that the drips collected from one tap during one week would fill a bathtub with water? It is important to make sure that a tap is turned off completely so water is not wasted.

△ In some countries, people do not have fresh water piped to their homes. They must carry water long distances in buckets.

Saving water at home

There are many ways for you and your family to save water at home. Have a quick shower instead of a bath. You will still be clean, but you will save water!

◁ Make sure that the washing machine or dishwasher is full before you turn it on. You will not need to use these machines as often.

If you pour yourself a drink of water, do not run the tap to make sure that the water is really cold. Add ice cubes to your glass or cool a jug of water in the fridge instead.

The small tank above a toilet is called a **cistern**. It is filled with water, which rushes down the toilet when you flush. When you put a special bag into the cistern, there is room for less water. You will use less water each time you flush the toilet.

FACT!

In 2000, power plants in the United States used about 136,000 million gallons of fresh water.

Saving water outside

Some people use huge amounts of water to keep their gardens green and healthy. By leaving a **water butt** or a bucket outside, you can collect rainwater when it rains and use the water when the weather is dry.

◁ A sprinkler can use as much water in one hour as a family of four uses in a whole day! Use a watering can instead of a sprinkler.

When it rains, put houseplants outside to soak up the water. You will not need to water the plants as often.

FACT!

If you remove weeds from the garden, other plants will be healthier and will need less water to grow.

△ If you like to grow plants, pick ones that do not need much water. A **cactus** needs hardly any water!

Saving water at school

At school, each student uses up to 4,000 liters of water a year—that is enough water to fill a bath every week! There are a lot of ways for schools and students to conserve water.

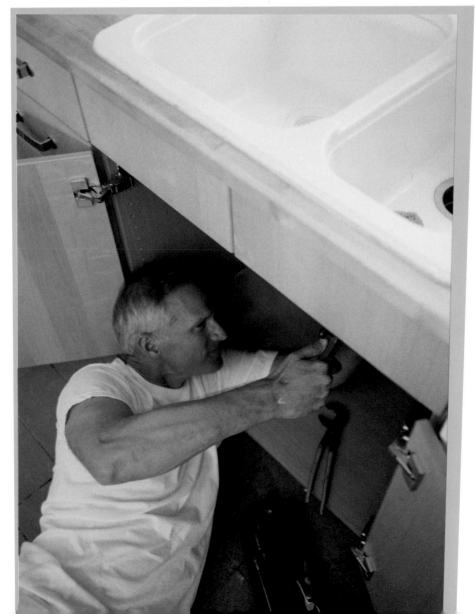

◁ If you see any leaky pipes, tell a teacher. Water companies can come and fix leaky pipes in the school or leaky pipes underground.

A **water meter** measures how much water is being used. Ask to check your school's water meter. You will then be able to see how much water you are saving!

△ Put a plug in the sink before you turn the tap on to wash your hands. The plug will prevent you from using more water than you need. When you have finished washing your hands, make sure you turn the taps off properly.

More ideas!

Rainwater harvesting is a way of collecting water. As rain falls on roofs, it pours into water butts or underground tanks. The rainwater can then be used for flushing the toilet, washing clothes, and watering the garden.

△ A water butt catches water that runs off the roofs of these huts in Belize.

Before you wash up, place a small bowl into a large sink. You will use less water when you wash up. If you are boiling a kettle, only pour in as much water as you need. You will use less water and the kettle will take less time to boil.

△ Use a bucket of water and a sponge to wash a car, instead of a hose. You will save liters of water.

Glossary

acid rain Polluted water that falls as rain

cactus A plant covered in prickles that grows in hot, dry places

chemicals Powerful liquids or powders that can be used for a lot of things, including cleaning

cistern A small tank of water above a toilet

coarse Made of large, rough pieces

dam A strong wall built across a river valley to hold back water

destroy To break or damage something so that it is beyond repair

droplet A tiny amount of liquid

environment Everything around us that affects how we live

factories Buildings where people make things with machines

flushed Washed away with water

germs Tiny living things that sometimes cause diseases

ground water Water that is found underground

piped When a liquid or gas is sent down a tube

pollution Dirty or unhealthy air, land, or water

population The number of people who live in a country or a place

reservoir A man-made lake

sewage plant A place where dirty toilet water is cleaned

sewers Pipes that take dirty toilet water away to sewage plants

submarine A ship that can travel underwater

surface The outside or top of something

valley A deep dip in the land, usually containing a flowing river

wastewater treatment works A place where dirty water is cleaned

water butt A large barrel that catches rainwater

water cycle How water moves around Earth

waterfall A stream or river of water falling from a high place to a low place

water vapor Tiny droplets of water in the air

well A hole dug to get water out of the ground

Index

Printed in the USA